FREE AT LAST!

FREE AT LAST!

Healing from the ravages of sexual abuse, and how to minister to those who have experienced it.

Cheryl ZumBrunnen

Printed in the United States of America.

ISBN 0-9704066-0-6

Printed in the United States by
Morris Publishing
3212 East Highway 30
Kearney, NE 68847
1-800-650-7888

*I dedicate this book to
my husband David, daughter Kristi, and son Shain.
They were the ones who lived with me through the
dark days of my healing process and
chose to love me anyway.*

*I give deep thanks to those who have
helped make this book possible.
Emily for editing, Kathy for typesetting, and
Barbara and Cheryl for content and spiritual guidance.
I would not be who I am, able to do what I do today,
without the influence and love of these extraordinary people.*

TABLE OF CONTENTS

INTRODUCTION

      This book is written from the heart of one who has experienced sexual abuse and has walked through the slow, painful healing process into the light, love and freedom offered through Jesus Christ. If you are a victim of sexual abuse, inside these pages you will find the hope, strength and tools to allow the Lord Jesus Christ to lead you into His promised protection, comfort and freedom. If you are a person who has never had to experience this violation, but you have a heartfelt desire to minister to and come alongside those who have, you will find insight, understanding and tools to use in doing so.

PREFACE

Being a full-time, Bible-based, Christian discipleship/counselor, I have the privilege of working with many people who have been sexually, emotionally, physically or mentally abused. Unfortunately, I find that, even though abuse counseling and support groups are available all over the country, many who have experienced one or more forms of abusive trauma have not found peace or freedom from the memories of their abuse through these avenues.

I believe that the ONLY way to lasting freedom from the effects of abuse is through the avenue of understanding one's identity in Christ Jesus, thereby having an unshakable foundation from which to process the abuse issues and replace the lies of the past with the truth of God. This type of discipleship/counseling offers clients an atmosphere of complete acceptance of them as individuals, and creates a safe environment in which they can tell their story without fear of condemnation or blame. The discipler's task is to keep pointing the victim back to Jesus and His unconditional love. The most important thing for an abused person is to have someone they can trust, and that someone is Jesus. He is the only person who will never let them down in some form or fashion.

I begin telling my story by sharing, in detail, my sexual-abuse experience. The reason I have been detailed about the acts committed against me is that, all too often, most persons who have been sexually abused feel that if they told the whole truth, omitting nothing about what happened, others would be condemning of them, or think they were just trying to get attention. When some abused persons hold in the details of the abuse, those details and the emotional pain connected with them come back to haunt them time and time again. When they are given the opportunity for a safe place to share everything, it can often bring a measure of freedom from the nightmarish memories. When all the facts are out in the open, the person is often more able to listen to godly counsel. They can no longer say, "But you don't really know what happened to me; how can you understand?" Sharing of the details of sexual abuse can also stop the misconception of some that if your experience wasn't as bad as mine, you don't have a right to be as devastated as I am; or just the opposite, if what happened to me wasn't as bad as what happened to you, then I must be wrong to feel so violated. It is also true that some victims of abuse do not need to share the intimate details of their experience to find true freedom. What I strive to do is work with the individual to facilitate a place of emotional and relational safety where they can work through their abuse experience(s) in the way that best meets their particular needs.

Statistics from the mid 90's state that one in four women in America, and one in six men, have been in some way sexually violated at some time in their life. I am one of those statistics. It is my prayer that those who read this will find the same healing and freedom as I did in the name and person of Jesus Christ.

PART I

Chapter

1 This Couldn't Have Happened To Me!

"Lord Jesus, You and I have been together for about four years now and I can't praise You enough for what You are doing in my life. You have saved my marriage, helped me to be a better mom, delivered me from the bondage of being a compulsive liar, and You have miraculously provided financially through my five major surgeries in these last four years! You truly are a God worthy to be worshipped and praised.

"Lord, I want to keep growing in my understanding of You. I do not want anything in my life that could be a hindrance or stumbling block between You and me. Reveal to me anything that may be hidden in secret so that the enemy, Satan, cannot use it against me. You said that it was for freedom that You have set me free. I want the fullness of freedom You offer."

A few days later I was driving down a busy street in my small Alaska town when my truck stalled at an intersection. No matter what I did, I could not get it to start. People were honking at me, and one man yelled a cutting remark out his window about women drivers. I turned on my flashing lights, walked across the street and called my husband to come and rescue me. He was not happy with the intrusion on his time, and grilled me to make sure I had tried all the usual things to get the truck to start. He told me to wait twenty minutes or so and call him back if the truck still wouldn't start.

By the time I got back in the truck I was really angry. Traffic was bottled up and I felt like a fool just sitting there. I found myself starting to cry.

"Oh, Cheryl, it's not that bad. The thing just won't start. There is nothing you can do about it so, calm down." I just cried harder. My self pep-talk didn't work.

It's hard to capture into words just what happened next.

As I sat there, crying out my frustration and anger, a picture came into my mind. It was pristine clear and undeniably real.

I was out in a hay field with a trusted friend of the family. I could feel the warmth of the summer sun on my three-year-old face. I was running and laughing as he chased me, thinking we were playing a game of tag. He caught me and held on as I squealed and playfully struggled to get away. He sat down on the ground and put me down beside him. I watched as he stood up again and proceeded to pull his pants down. He told me to do the same.

I could hear myself protesting because I didn't want the Alaskan divebomber mosquitoes to get me. His voice was soft and soothing. He pulled me to a standing position beside him, unhooked and pulled down my overalls. He began to run his hands all over my private parts. I tried to pull away. I told him I didn't like this game. He took a firm hold on my arm, and with his other hand, continued fondling me. He was hurting me. He wouldn't stop. I became angry and scared and started to cry. When I wouldn't stop crying he became gruff with me. He must have been afraid someone would hear, as my house was not too far away. He got up, pulled his pants up and walked off, leaving me there undressed and crying.

As I sat there in my stalled truck, hysterically crying, I felt like a fool. I knew that those driving around me would think I had lost my mind!

I cried out to God, begging Him to reassure me that this was just a hallucination. I pleaded with Him to make it go away. This couldn't have happened to me!

I was in shock! An hour before, if someone had asked me if I had ever been sexually molested in any way, at any time in my life, I would have said unequivocally NO, and truly believed it.

I don't know how long I sat there crying. I could not get the horrible scene out of my mind. I could not understand how someone who had been a good friend of our family, and who had acted as though he was committed to loving and protecting me, could do such a thing to an innocent little girl. My emotions were charging through rage, hate and disgust to the point of feeling like I would vomit. I imagined the perpetrator tied to a tree while I beat his face in!

Why had he gotten away with it? He deserved to be punished! How many other little girls had he violated through the years? "Oh, Lord! Where is the justice I read about in Your Word for me, and most of all, against him?"

"Jesus, where were you? Why did you let this happen to me? You promised to protect the little ones from harm and violation!"

In the midst of my outburst these words came to mind as the Lord reminded me of my recent prayer.

"Cheryl, remember a few days ago when you asked Me to reveal anything hidden in secret that could be a potential stumbling block in your relationship with Me? Remember that freedom you asked for? This is the answer to your prayer. Don't be bitter. Forgive this person so you can truly taste the freedom I have for you."

It had only been a matter of about thirty minutes since the memory had flooded my consciousness. How could I already be at the point of being asked to forgive? Forgiveness had been the topic of my women's Bible study for the last several weeks. I knew what forgiveness was, why we are asked by God to do it, and how to do it. It was a fresh topic in my mind, and I assume that is why God was able to bring it up at this point in my process. Even so, I was shocked at the idea.

"FORGIVE HIM! YOU'VE GOT TO BE KIDDING! HE DOESN'T DESERVE TO BE FORGIVEN! HE DESERVES TO BE LOCKED UP IN JAIL AND HAVE THE KEY THROWN AWAY!"

I sensed the presence of God with me and was gently reminded by Him of what I had learned about forgiveness. "The forgiveness is not for him, Cheryl, it is for you. You are the one who prayed for freedom. You are the one I want to set free. He is my responsibility. I have, I am, and I will deal with him."

I had never experienced such intense emotions in my life. It was frightening. I felt myself losing total control. If the emotions became any more intense, I was afraid I would never be able to stop them. I cried out to the Lord to help me deal with this gross violation of my being. I had experienced enough of Christ's love and goodness to know that I could trust Him. And yet, it was all happening so fast.

It wasn't until many months later that I realized there had been nothing fast about it. There had been over twenty years of silent suffering filled with glaring, confusing consequences. In many ways it was a blessing to have the abuse dealt with in this way. Unknown to me, God had been preparing me for this moment during all of those years. Because of His loving presence and preparation, I was able to stumble through those first wrenching minutes and the days that followed.

I kept praying, asking God to enable me to choose to forgive the one who violated me. "Lord Jesus, I cannot do this on my own. I cannot even do this with Your help! You are going to have to forgive him for me, through me. I meant it when I told You I wanted Your freedom. I don't want anything in my life that would hinder our relationship. Even though I am hurting beyond anything I ever imagined, I am going to thank You for revealing this secret to me. I thank You that You will give me Your strength to deal with it. And Lord, I choose to forgive him. I release him to You. After all, none of this was hidden in secret from You. From the little I know about this man's life, I know that he has suffered much. I want for him what You want for him, salvation through forgiveness."

I don't know how long it took for me to come to this point of decision. I was sure that this was where the Lord was leading me and I knew it was right. I was still in shock and the emotional pain was no less, but I was also at peace in my spirit. I knew I had obeyed the Scripture by choosing to forgive, even though what I really wanted was revenge. I reached down, turned the key in the ignition, the motor burst to life and I drove home.

I had been sitting at the intersection for less than one hour.

2 REFLECTIONS

I was raised in a loving family. My father was a railroad worker and had to be gone from home a great deal of the time. Yet I never lacked for his love and attention. He succeeded in creating a feeling of security for me even though he wasn't there. I say "he," but as I look back, I can see that it was both my mother and my father working together who created my secure home life. Mother was a stay-at-home mom while I was growing up. She made sure that my sister, brother and I were well taken care of and loved. She always included Daddy in our lives. When we would ask permission to go do something with friends she would answer, "I think Dad and I could let you do that." They were a team even when he wasn't there. As I replay my childhood memories, I see now how precious that stability was and the important role it played in my upbringing.

There was also a dark side to my childhood. I was an overweight child. I was the brunt of a lot of name-calling from my classmates at school. "Here comes Cheryl the barrel," or "Fatty, fatty two-by-four, can't get through the kitchen door," and any other ones that come to your mind as you read these. It hurt. We had a small school and there was no place to hide. The bright spot through all of this was my best friend. She liked me; no, she loved me. We really were good for each other. If it hadn't been for Linda, I don't know what I would have done. I know now that it was because of her friendship in elementary and junior high that I was included in the cool parties with the popular kids.

I had one other thing going for me in school, and that was my musical ability. I played the piano and the clarinet, but my real plus was my voice. My father, sister and I started singing trios in church when I was about eight years old. That was where I received the most strokes. People were always praising me, even on the street. They never said anything about how fat I was, just how well I could sing. I drank in this praise like a desert traveler dying of thirst. Every pore in my being thirsted after more and more avenues of recognition. I was consumed with searching for ways to fit in and feel accepted.

In elementary school I was the class clown along with two other boys. We could be counted on to disrupt just about anything, anytime. I was known in junior high and high school as the person who could yell the loudest at the basketball games, much to my voice teacher's dismay. This honor gave me the esteemed position of being the cheerleading mascot. When I was a senior in high school the music teacher became very ill. I was asked by the principal to teach the music classes until he was well enough to return. I was to teach not only the high school band and chorus, but the elementary grades as well. This was the ultimate glory for me! I was elevated to a position of authority and power, and I relished the esteem given me by my peers. Don't ask me how it happened, but I eventually ended up with the captain of the basketball team as my boyfriend! These events and relationships fed my ego to the max, for a while.

I was obsessed with losing weight. I spent a good part of my life on one diet or another. I was very creative and developed many of my own special diets, convinced that each one would be the one to end all diets. I was a pro at losing weight, but I was an even more successful pro at gaining it back. The only time I can remember being at an acceptable weight was when I was a sophomore in high school and contracted the "kissing disease," mononucleosis. I spent time in the hospital and many months gaining my strength back, as well as the weight I had lost during the illness.

As I reminisce about the "good old days," I see that my life consisted of doing everything I could to lose weight and hating myself as I gained it back. I spent many sleepless nights devising new ways to cover up my feelings of inadequacy, inferiority and failure, while planning my next "last-time-I'll-ever-have-to-diet" diet.

These behaviors carried over into college. I only went to college because I didn't know what else to do. My sister and brother were both in college and doing well, so I decided to try it too.

I was scared to death, but wasn't about to let anyone know it. I enrolled in a two-year business program and had flunked out by the end of the year. This failure impacted my life with a force I could not contend with. I stuffed my emotions and blamed the professors for not liking me. I came back next fall and enrolled in a music education program thinking this would be the thing to vindicate me in the eyes of my peers and the school. I saw right away that my musical ability was not looked upon by the college staff with the same awe I had experienced in high school and church. My insecurities drove me to new heights in trying to get noticed. The problem was that all my antics did was cause my college peers and professors to think of me as a "flake."

I met David in the university choir, and we were married the summer following my sophomore year. We returned to college that fall. I was now a full-time employed wife enrolled in college. I was doing a miserable job at all three roles and felt frantic. My solution was to give up college and direct my full energy into being a wife. Oh, I had to keep the job, but that was a necessary evil in my life. I was now focused on being super wife!

I had no idea at the time how insecure I was about myself, or that I had zero self-worth. I see now that I centered my young life on doing everything I could to remain Linda's friend and to use my musical ability to get attention whenever possible. After high school I tapped into my natural verbal skills that allowed me to talk circles around most people, usually enabling me to manipulate others so that I could end up the one in the limelight. I see in hindsight that I was doing whatever I had to do to maintain control of my circumstances and relationships in order to get attention, with the goal of somehow feeling acceptable. I had no idea that I was on an emotional treadmill that was leading nowhere.

Chapter

3 Processing ...

In the weeks after I remembered the sexual abuse, I walked in a daze. I mustered up the strength to tell my husband what had happened. He was everything I needed him to be. He comforted me, loved me, cried with me and talked with me for hours on end. Through the conversations the Lord began unraveling all the consequences this act had brought about in my life, the things I mentioned before.

I can remember feeling that I had been cheated out of my innocence. I was so angry and hurt. We didn't know where to turn. We thought of going to our pastor for help, but I was too humiliated. So David and I tried walking through this season alone.

WHAT A MISTAKE! I was depressed; I didn't know it, but that didn't stop me from acting it out! I was very short-tempered with, and had very high expectations of, my two little children and my husband, not to mention myself.

I had been a performance-oholic all my life, but now that was intensified a thousand-fold. I was already involved in almost everything our little church and community had to offer. When these involvements were not enough of a distraction I began inventing more projects in which to become absorbed. My life-long, uncontrollable need to prove myself to be "okay," or acceptable, intensified. The problem with this goal was that I had no idea what "okay" looked or felt like. I could never be sure whether I had reached the goal, because I had no definition of the term. I became a strict, controlling, obnoxious person to be around at home. I had the same characteristics in public, but I knew how to sugar-coat and hide them in order to get my way. I had to have all the recognition and praise I could get. I became a master at manipulating others for my benefit. I had a huge empty hole in my being that craved affirmation, yet there never seemed to be enough to fill it up.

I hated being at home with the children because they demanded so much of my mental and emotional energy. I invented things to go do just so I could drop the kids off at grandma's. Thank God she loved having them. At one point in my process I somehow managed to worm my way into some position of leadership in fourteen different committees and organizations. I was never home because I couldn't stand being with myself, coping with the responsibility of my children or facing the reality that I was not "super wife," and never would be.

In short, I was a walking emotional time bomb, wanting desperately to believe that God loved me as much as He said He did in the Bible, and that that love would somehow break through my pain and set me free. I wanted to believe it, but had no resources to do so.

4 SLOW DEATH

During the two years following the revelation of the sexual abuse, I had been attending a women's Bible study. I was convinced the woman leading was a fake, yet I kept going back. She was always telling us how the Lord had done this or that for her because she had prayed and asked Him to meet her every need according to His plan for her life. I was doing the very same thing every day, and nothing was changing in my life. Well, that is not really true: I was becoming more and more miserable. I was reading my Bible and doing everything I could to believe God's promises, but without any improvement.

I was on a frantic search for the one promise that kept eluding me, no matter what I did or how hard I prayed—the promise of peace of mind. I was begging and bargaining with God to make this elusive condition real in my life. The more I begged, the more despondent I became. The more depressed I became, the more driven I was to prove to the Lord, the world, and myself that I was "okay."

The day finally came when I gave in to my misery and doubt and fearfully admitted I was angry with Jesus. That was a scary thing for me. I had been taught that it was wrong to be angry. It was ingrained in me that being angry with God was a sin. SIN! Yet it was true. What was I supposed to do about it? Oh, I knew I had given Him permission to reveal anything hidden in secret in my life...but THIS? My cry was, "Lord! This is so painful! Couldn't You have done something else? What could be the purpose for my going through all this pain?"

Feeling strung out and full of fear, plagued by unanswered questions, I dragged myself to Bible study. I was doing my best to put on my usual confident air of being in control. I was scared to death that I wouldn't be able to maintain the mask for very long. All the while I was thinking, "What if these women find out that I'm a fake? I could never handle that!"

A FAKE? Where did that come from? A fake? I had never thought of myself that way before; why now?

"The Scripture lesson for today," began the Bible study leader, "is found in 1 Thessalonians 5:16-18. 'Be joyful always; pray continually; give thanks in all circumstances, for this is God's will for you in Christ Jesus.' What does this mean to you?"

I almost came out of my seat. "You've got to be kidding! I have been praying constantly, that's for sure. But rejoicing? Giving thanks?" My cool, well-practiced mask of self-control broke into a thousand pieces. There was a raging war going on in me. How could Jesus ask me to praise Him in the midst of this debilitating pain? It isn't fair! I wasn't the one who had sinned against me! I had been the innocent victim, not the perpetrator!

With as much composure as I could muster, I quietly gathered up my Bible and purse and tiptoed out of the room, feeling as though I would faint from the effort.

The days that followed this encounter with the living God were wrenching. My search for that mysterious commodity known as "the peace that passes understanding" consumed my waking hours. At night it was always just out of reach in my tormented dreams.

As I search my memories of that time in my life, I am overcome with the Lord's grace to me and my family during those dark days.

David was doing his best to understand me. Yet, the more he tried, the more I pulled away. I was incapable of receiving his love and affection. In truth, I could not stand to have him near me physically or emotionally. I knew, and he knew, that what was going on with me had nothing to do with him. This should

15

have been a comfort to both of us. But, instead, it was total frustration for David, and a source of increasing guilt for me.

I would spend the whole day talking myself through my feelings and telling myself that it was silly to reject David when he was not the one who had hurt me. I would take time to shower, dress nicely, and dab on just the right amount of sweet smelling-cologne. I would believe I had convinced myself that David and I could enjoy an intimate evening together, forgetting what had happened.

David would come home, always on edge, wondering what kind of a mood I would be in. He would see me looking relaxed and receptive and the tension in his face would melt. But, no matter how hard I tried to keep up the front, when the evening would wind down and we were headed to the bedroom, I'd freeze, unable to follow through with my fantasy. The only fruit of this torturous treadmill was the successful increase of my exhausting guilt.

This became a pattern in our marriage that led me into a deep depression filled with hopelessness. I was trapped. My tread-mill had no "off" switch!

I wish I could tell you that within a short while the Lord, in his mercy, healed me from my "victim complex" and life be-came a joy. I WISH! The opposite was true. I was consumed with my "pity party" life style. To make matters more complicated, this was not the only trauma I was dealing with in my life.

During this time, David became enthralled with the sport of dog sledding. It came at a good time for him. Our marriage was at the point that, in my opinion, he could do nothing right, so dog sledding became his life. He could be out enjoying him-self and not have to be around me. I couldn't blame him. Never-theless, I was dealing with major feelings of rejection. He was never around. I had been upstaged by a bunch of dogs!

Another stressful situation was my small son's health. He was not well. He had not been well since birth. I knew some-thing was wrong with him but I could not get our local doctors to listen to me. I was told that I was an over-protective mother. I was told that his symptoms were the classic symptoms of an unloved child. I was frantic! In other words, it was all MY fault. It was my fault that he could not keep any food down. It was my fault that he cried all the time because he was so miserable. It was my fault that he never slept unless he was being held in an upright position.

Then there was my daughter. She was healthy, happy and being profoundly ignored because she did not have any glaring needs—that is, of course, unless you count the need to be loved and included in my life. In short, I felt that I was a rotten mother and wife. I added these failures to my "guilty-as-charged" list and became increasingly more depressed.

Remember I was still running the church and community, too. Leadership in those fourteen different committees or organizations, and the continued frenzied search for more ways to prove my worth, were taking their toll. My body was reacting to the severe stress in my life. I was in the midst of undergoing a series of five major surgeries in seven years. Now you have a pretty clear picture of my sad, miserable existence.

Through all of this, God had become my "911," my rescue squad. On the days when I was so overwhelmed that I thought I would literally explode from the stress, I would call out to God. Bless Him, He was always there. I say that, not because I had a deep sense of His presence or His peace, but because He always enabled me to wake up the next morning to do it all over again.

I was still in the women's Bible study. That truly was the grace of God! Every time I would get ready to go I would fight with myself. "Why are you doing this, Cheryl? None of the things that she says are true in your life. Jesus isn't supplying all your needs. If He were, your son wouldn't be sick; David wouldn't be absent from your life." But, I would still go. I know that part of the reason I went was that I could drop the children at my mother's and be free from the demands of my son for a few hours. It was a purely selfish motive for going anywhere. Mom was always ready, willing and eager to have her grandchildren. I was always ready, willing and eager to be free of the responsibility of them for a while. It worked out well for all concerned.

5 WELCOME DEATH

The harder I tried to prove my worth, the harder it became to find ways to try to prove my worth. I knew I was failing miserably and would never reach my goal. I was dead inside. I had no emotions to give to anyone. "If this is the way life is going to be, then I don't want to live it." This thought became more and more prevalent in my thinking. I would catch myself during the midnight hours holding my son, my arms and back aching from the strain, thinking of different ways I had heard of that people had committed suicide. Guns? Too messy; I could never do it that way. Asphyxiation? I would probably chicken out halfway through that one. Hanging? I couldn't figure out how I would do it. Pills? Yes, pills seemed to be the easiest and least messy way to remove myself from the constant pain in my being. Then I would think about what kind of pills, and where I could get them.

"HOLD IT! What are you thinking, Cheryl? Christians are not supposed to commit suicide. God would definitely reject you if you did that!" Then I would think, "I already feel completely rejected by God, so what's the big deal?"

Yet, like a dream encased in thick fog, there was a vague memory of a time when I did feel close to God—a distant time when I knew He was real and important in my life. The truth was, I already felt completely abandoned by God; but to be totally rejected by Him? As I stood staring at the various bottles of pills in the medicine cabinet, I couldn't help wondering: What had happened? Where had He gone? Why was His voice absent from my mind?

Chapter
6 PROPER BURIAL

These questions plagued me day and night. I couldn't understand why the Lord was being so silent. I had run out of things to do to try to recapture the closeness. My guilt was telling me that I must have done something unforgivable for Him to be treating me so brutally. I was consumed with despair.

Through all of these trials I was still trying to be the model Christian. So, on this particular day, like most other days, I sat down at the kitchen table with my Bible and my prayer journal to have my quiet time with the Lord. HA! It was a quiet time, all right; I couldn't tell that God took part at all.

I sat there, trying to get in the right frame of mind by reading some of the praise Psalms. That didn't work. I tried thanking the Lord for what He was doing in my life. That for sure didn't work! My frustration level was at the boiling point. I started wondering why I even cared any more what God thought of me. Obviously He didn't care for me very much, so I decided just to stop caring for Him.

I was so angry that I picked up my Bible and threw it across the room. It splattered against the far wall, papers and notes flying everywhere, and hit the floor with a dead thud. "Jesus, I'm done! Finished! If this is what the abundant Christian life is all about, you can have it! I can do this well on my own, and that is just what I feel like I have been doing! It's over! You do Your thing and I'll do mine from now on!"

I don't know how long I sat at the table, numb inside. I was completely empty and abandoned. When my tears were almost spent and I was wondering what to do next, I sensed the presence of another person in the room. Just as I was about to turn my head to see who it was, I heard a soft, intense voice exclaim, "Finally!"

I froze in place. I instantly recognized the voice from past conversations. Hope began to rise in me. After all this time, was it really Him?

I didn't turn around. I didn't have to. I knew that I had just heard the voice of the Lord sounding sweet and confident in my ear, like when I first knew Him.

The time span was far too short for any of my circumstances to have changed, yet I had an acute sense of the all-encompassing presence of the Lord within me. He had not abandoned me after all! Still, I could not shake the feeling of dread. I was acutely aware of His presence and fearful of what He might say to me.

"O Lord! It has been so long since You have talked to me. I was so afraid that You were gone from my life forever. I know I have made a royal mess of everything, and I wouldn't blame You if You were here to tell me it was over for You, too."

I was overcome with grief and guilt. I just knew it was all over between Jesus and me, and it was all my fault, as usual. In tearful anguish I sat with my head in my hands, waiting for that sweet voice to confirm my worst fears.

Chapter

7 Joyful Resurrection

To my astonishment, a supernatural calm came over my being. I felt as if the weight of a thousand pounds had been lifted off my back. I was exhausted, yet exhilarated. What was happening? I was afraid to believe what I was sensing. I was engulfed in what I could only call "the peace that passes understanding." For the first time in several years my mind was at rest. This was so foreign to my existence that I was afraid to believe it.

A conversation began to take shape in my thoughts between my Savior and me.

Jesus: "Cheryl, this is not the first time in the past several years of pain that I have talked to you. However, it is the first time in these last several years that you have been still enough to listen. You have been so busy running your own life I could not get a word in edgewise. Now listen to me. Did you, or did you not, invite Me to come into your life?"

Cheryl: "Yes, Lord, I did."

Jesus: "Then you are My child, My daughter. Do you believe that?"

Cheryl: "Yes, Lord, I do."

Jesus: "Okay then, here is how it is going to be from now on. You are to accept everything, WITHOUT EXCEPTION, that comes into your life from Me. It doesn't matter if it feels bad, good, or indifferent; just claim it from Me. Then, when it is not from Me, I WILL TELL YOU. I will not take credit for anything that is not Mine. When your own selfish desires and will are trying to take over again, don't worry; I'll tell you. When your enemy, Satan, is trying to harass you, don't worry; I'll tell you.

STOP TRYING TO DO MY JOB! I am the one who will guide and direct your thoughts and actions. I never go back on My Word. Trust Me to do just as I have promised."

Cheryl: "Lord, I thought that was what I was trying to do. What changed that I am sensing Your presence and hearing Your voice in my mind so clearly now?"

Jesus: "You gave up. You 'threw in the towel,' so to speak. You finally came to the end of your own schemes and abilities to try, one more time, to make life work on your own. I have not been silent, Cheryl; you have chosen not to listen. Today you came to the end of your own resources and gave up. This opened the way for Me to be heard."

Cheryl: "Okay Lord; I am not sure I really understand what You are telling me, but I desperately want to. I don't want this season in my life to be repeated, ever! Please teach me so that I will have a clear grasp of all that has happened and why. I still don't know who I am, Lord. I do know that what happened today was true, and that You are here with me. My fear is that it won't last. I am afraid that I will do or not do something that will cause You to become silent again. I couldn't bear that, Lord! Help me! Where do we go from here?"

Jesus: "DO NOTHING! That has been the problem! You have been searching for My peace, acceptance and love by trying to meet your own needs out of your own resources. It is a lie that you have to do something in order to be acceptable to Me. You are one hundred percent acceptable to Me, just because I say so. You didn't do anything to make this true, and you cannot do anything that will cause it to become untrue. I freely died so that you might live. I did everything that needed to be done. It is a finished script. All you need to do is learn your part as I wrote it, and act out your role with enthusiasm."

My head was spinning. What did all of this mean?

Chapter

8 NOW I GET IT!

It took several months, and the counsel of numerous godly people, for this new revelation to unravel in my brain. As I look back, I am awed at the Lord's patience. It just seemed too good to be true. I had been taught in church all my life that I was to "work" out my faith with fear and trembling. To me that meant that if I didn't perform just right, the Lord would reject me. I thought I was supposed to be afraid of God and His wrath so that I would not give up trying to work out my salvation. In other words, fear of God, and fear of being rejected by God and others, was the primary motivation in my life.

It is really true that hindsight is twenty-twenty. My hindsight was revealing to me a clear picture of how close God had been to me during the hard times.

One of His clear acts of closeness was keeping me going to the women's Bible study. It was through the leader that I learned of Philippines 2:12-13. "Therefore, my dear friends, as you have always obeyed - not only in my presence, but now much more in my absence - continue to work out your salvation with fear and trembling, for it is God who works in you to will and to act according to His good purpose."

Wow! There were those words that had tripped me up my whole Christian life. The Bible study leader took the time to talk me through Philippians, chapters one and two, so I would have the full understanding of the whole meaning of those words.

I was so relieved! I no longer had to be afraid of the Lord. He said He would never reject me. He does not lie. I had completely misunderstood this Scripture passage.

The key that unlocked my understanding came in chapter two, verse 13. "...For it is *God* who works in you (in me) to will (to decide) and to act (to put into action) according to *His* good purpose." This was confirmation of what I had heard the Lord say to me the day I gave up. He will call the shots. I won't have to! He really can be trusted to make it all work together for my good (Romans 8:28). He will work out His good purpose through me for the good of others and myself. Yes, I am to "do" work in the kingdom, but not for the purpose of earning Jesus' love or acceptance. The acts I carry out are to be the *product* of my relationship with Him, not the *basis* of that relationship.

Okay, let's see if I understand this now: 1) I cannot earn Jesus' love, because it is a free gift given to me, by Him (John 3:16-17); 2) I cannot perform well enough to be acceptable to the Lord, because He accepted me one hundred percent before I was formed in my mother's womb (Romans 15:7; Psalm 139:13-16); 3) It is God, not me, who works in me and through me so that I will be able to know His will and act accordingly (Romans 12:1-2); 4) All of this is so that *His* good purposes will be carried out through my life (Galatians 2:20; Philippians 2:13) ; and 5) I need to choose to allow Jesus, through the person of the Holy Spirit, to live His life through me, "...so that you (I) may become blameless and pure, children of God without fault in a crooked and depraved generation, in which you (I) shine like stars in the universe as you (I) hold out the word of life..." (Philippians 2:14-15).

Now I get it! Jesus will decide what, how, when, where and why something is to take place, and all I have to do is be the vessel through which He will carry it out.

All this time I really had been trying to do His job. I was so consumed with trying to be pleasing to God and others so I could feel acceptable, that I got in my own way and hindered my ability to hear God's voice and follow it. I was trying to be God! What a really warped thing to do! No wonder I was such an emotional and relational mess.

Chapter

9 APPLICATION PROCESS

I was like a kid with my own candy store! I had never known such freedom. For the first time in my life I had a solid knowledge of who I was. I was lovable and acceptable, and there wasn't anything I could ever do that would change that.

As I began to concentrate on these freeing truths, I realized that the Lord had given me a wonderful sabbatical from my troubles. He had given me time to digest His banquet of blessings before He asked me to face the issue of the sexual abuse once again.

I hadn't thought about the abuse for several months, and was very surprised when it surfaced again. I admit I was afraid. This was the test. Could I hang onto my new-found freedom and finish the process of dealing with the abuse? Wasn't it the opening up of the memory that had caused me to go through those years of pain and grief?

The answer to that question was, "no." It was the initial event that had begun my path of self-consumption. My little three-year-old mind couldn't comprehend the abuse and therefore buried it deep within me. Nevertheless, the abuse had a profound effect on my whole being. Because of the emotional violation, the need to prove myself "okay" had become the controlling factor in my life.

The act of violation against my body communicated to my mind and emotions that I must have done something wrong for my friend to treat me that way. After all, he had liked me before that happened, and would hardly come around me afterward. Unconsciously, I believed this lie about myself and began the all-consuming search for ways to prove it wasn't true.

I came before the Lord and agreed with Him that the abuse issue was still unfinished business in my life. I asked the Lord to show me how to deal with this issue out of the foundation of what I now knew to be the truth about myself.

God began to show me that I had been living my life based on a series lie.

Lie: I must have done something wrong to cause my friend to treat me that way.

Truth: I did not do anything wrong. The perpetrator was totally at fault for what he did to me. I was an innocent three-year-old child.

Lie: I became unacceptable and unlovable to God, myself and others because I was sexually abused.

Truth: I am, I have always been, and I will always be one hundred percent acceptable and unconditionally loved by God, in Christ. Because of this truth, when others act toward me as though I am not acceptable to them, I can continue to love them, because my worth is based not on what they think of me, but on my oneness with Christ Jesus.

Lie: I have to be involved in as many Christian programs as possible in order to prove my self-worth.

Truth: My worth ONLY comes from Jesus Christ. It is a free gift He gave me. I cannot earn it, and I cannot un-earn it by my actions.

Lie: I must not have really forgiven the man who abused me, because I was still emotionally distraught over the incident.

Truth: Forgiveness is not based on emotions. It is a conscious act of the will. It is making the choice to bring your will in line with God's will (Matthew 6:9-15). Then you ask the Lord to heal the emotions and bring them in line with the decision to forgive.

This error of associating forgiveness with emotions is where I got into trouble. I had never experienced such intense emotions. When the memory surfaced in me, twenty-two years' worth of emotional build-up assaulted my being all at once. I was overtaken by the sudden unleashing of all those intense feelings and didn't comprehend the full impact they would have on my life. I clearly made the decision to forgive the perpetrator, totally distinct from my emotional state. Yet, having had no experience with that level of emotional upheaval, I unknowingly jumped on the emotional roller coaster and had the most frightening, painful ride of my life. Feelings of inadequacy, insecurity, self-contempt, worthlessness and fear of failure were intensified tenfold. My life-controlling need to prove myself "okay" became an unquenchable obsession. This obsession ran my life until I could no longer contrive any other way to make life happen and gave up trying. Praise God for that day!

Lie: If you haven't forgotten about the sexual abuse, you haven't forgiven the perpetrator.

Truth: NO! God says He will forget your sins when you confess them (Jeremiah 31:34b). Nowhere in the Bible does it say that people will, should, or even can forget the sins committed against them or by them. However, the event and the emotions connected with it are not to control us.

As I shared, the emotional intensity at the beginning was overwhelming, but today it is not. This takes time. The greater the violation, the longer it takes to quiet the emotions surrounding it. Time, prayer and a growing intimacy with the Lord are the healers of emotions.

Lie: The time will come when you will never again adversely react to the memory of the abuse.

Truth: Time will dull the reaction to the memory of the abuse. Intense trauma leaves an imprint on a person's life which will never completely go away. The good news is that once people understand who they are in Christ, they can always depend on Him to lessen the shadow of the memory with His unconditional love, abounding mercy and grace.

Even though I was a believer in Jesus Christ as my Lord and Savior, I was still living my life based on the lies of my past. This was partly because I wasn't aware I was living a lie, and partly because it was the only way I knew how to live. I had not had the opportunity to be discipled by other Christians who understood their identity and could pass it on. I had been discipled by Christians who were doing just what I was, performing in order to feel acceptable.

The other dynamic of a lie-based belief system is that Satan will "salt" [compound] the lies we believe in order to further draw our attention away from God's love and grace. He uses the same tactics on us that he used on Adam and Eve. "Cheryl, are you sure God said... He loves you unconditionally, that you are acceptable to Him?" Because of my feelings that agreed with these doubts I kept trying harder and harder to prove myself "okay" with no success in sight. Is it any accident that in the book of John it says that we will know the truth and the truth will make us free? Living out of a truth-based belief system has truly brought the freedom and peace I so longed for, because it is God's truth and can not be altered by me in any way. I have no control over God, thank God! He made a decision to love me no matter what. I am thankful that I was able to make the decision to love myself as He loves me. Often my emotions don't agree with that decision, but so what! I am gaining more and more success at not letting my emotions control my thoughts and actions, thereby experiencing a greater measure of peace in my daily life and relationships.

Chapter

10 "I Do"

I want to take time to address the issue of relationships. Women, and men for that matter, who have been sexually violated, consistently have a very hard time entering into the long-term, intimate, sexual relationship in marriage.

I shared some of what was going on between my husband and me when the whole incident came to light. Things went from bad to worse.

The harder I tried to prove myself, the more I pulled away from David. I became so absorbed in myself that there was no room for anyone else in my life. I spent a great deal of time trying to talk myself into not blaming David for what had happened to me. After all, he was not the one who had abused me. He had always been tender and considerate with me during our intimate times together. I felt so guilty because I was so fickle. Once in a while I would be able to jump into his arms and allow him to love me, emotionally and physically, and it would be as it should be between husband and wife. Unfortunately, the norm was just the opposite. David could reach out for me in bed, the same way he had done a thousand times, and I would throw up my arms, shrink back and harshly push him away. Or worse yet, I would lie there, stiff as a board, wanting to scream, allowing him to touch me because I had decided that that was a wife's duty. David would ask me if it was all right to proceed, and I would lie to him and say, "yes." Poor guy, how was he supposed to know? The worst times were when my emotions were running high with indignation because of the abuse. I would lose the ability to separate the similarity in physical touch from the person doing it, and David became the abuser in my mind.

This was a constant battle for David, too. He was doing his best to understand my needs and respond to them, without taking my fickleness personally. He never put demands on me. I did that enough for both of us. I would set a standard of behavior that I thought was necessary for a wife, and then beat myself up when I couldn't live up to the standard. I didn't understand that I was emotionally beating up my husband as well. It was impossible for me to believe that he loved me just the way I was. I would not allow myself to receive his words or actions of love because I loathed myself. I felt dirty. I could not understand why he would want to make love to a person who was as detestable as I. My mind and emotions were so twisted that I felt I couldn't trust him because he didn't feel about me as I did.

I would like to tell you that on the day I gave up trying to run my own life and let Jesus take His rightful place as Lord, all of the problems with intimacy suddenly evaporated. I'd like to, but I can't.

For a woman, sexual intimacy is the frosting on the cake of marriage. When a woman feels loved, appreciated and honored by her spouse she is usually very willing to respond appropriately in the bedroom. But for a woman who has been sexually violated it is a much more complex issue than that. Her opinion of herself plays a big part in her ability to be sexually intimate.

As the Lord was ministering to me and I was beginning to understand my oneness with Christ, I began to be able to relax with David a little more. I was still upset because I did not feel free to accept his love, or freely to give love to him. I was still struggling with the fact that I didn't like myself. I was overweight and very insecure in relation to what others thought of me. I never allowed myself to see my whole body in the mirror. I was embarrassed when it wasn't pitch dark if we were making love, because I didn't want David to see me either. I was sure he would be repulsed by what he saw and never want to be with me again.

One day as I was praying about this issue I heard the Lord ask me to go stand in front of the full-length mirror in my bedroom. I reluctantly obeyed. My first reaction was one of disgust. As I stood there, the Lord began to fill my mind with what He thought of me.

I was created in the image of God (Genesis 1:26-27). His image? Does that mean that I look like Him? I have always thought of God as being beautiful and myself as being ugly.

I am God's workmanship, created in Christ Jesus (Ephesians 2:10). In the margin of my Bible I have written next to that verse that the Greek word for workmanship means, "a work of art." Does that mean that I am uniquely and deliberately created to be just the way I am? I sincerely hoped not!

God planned what I would look like, what family I would be born into, and what things I would accomplish in the kingdom, in His name, before I was formed in my mother's womb (Psalm 139:13-16).

I suddenly realized that God had left nothing to chance. I was not an accident. Nothing in my life was an accident or a surprise to God. If all the days ordained for me were planned by God before I was conceived, I must play an important part in His overall plan for mankind.

Does this mean that the sexual abuse was planned by God? No! God's plan for me was for good, not evil. A man planned my sexual abuse. A man committed the act of sexual violation against me. Long before it happened God had the plan in place that would turn it for good (Genesis 50:20; Romans 8:28).

"All right, Lord, I accept these things about me from You. I admit that I have not thought of myself in this way, even though I have heard all of these things time and time again. So what is it that is going to make the difference in me, enabling me really to believe these facts and act on them this time? How is it going to change my relationship with David?"

"Cheryl, why would you want to subject someone you love to having an intimate relationship with someone you despise?" My heart constricted as these words formed in my mind.

"OH.......................LORD! You really have a way of cutting to the chase. You're right. I would never encourage someone I love to be involved with someone I despise."

The choice I was faced with was choosing not to despise myself. This is not easily done, unless your strength comes from the Lord. God had brought me right back to the truths and lies I thought I had dealt with.

Lie: I am unacceptable because I feel unacceptable to myself.

Truth: I am one hundred percent acceptable, period—no ifs, ands, or buts about it.

My job was to act out the truth, and give God time to bring my emotions into agreement with my decision. One way I acted it out was to stand in front of the mirror each day and tell myself the truth about myself. This was one of the hardest things I had ever done in my life. I began doing it with my eyes closed because I couldn't stand to look at myself. As I began to speak the truth, little by little I started opening my eyes more and more. I would repeat over and over, "I am unconditionally loved and I am one hundred percent acceptable." I began to search the Scripture for more verses to back up these truths and was excited to find many more things that were true about myself. In short, I finally grasped the concept that whatever was true about Jesus was true about me. If it is no longer I who live now, but Christ who lives in me and through me, and if whatever happens in my life is from Him, and if I am only His arms, legs and mouthpiece, then He, Jesus Christ, dwells in His fullness in me. Then Jesus has the freedom to live His life through me, even in the bedroom (Colossians 2:9; Galatians 2:20).

I know it was an inspiration from the Lord, but a few days later I came up with the idea of changing my vocabulary to agree with what I understood the Lord to be encouraging me to do. I started saying, "Lord, what would you like to wear today?" "What would You like for breakfast?" "I can tell that David is looking for a little lovin' tonight, and I am not sure I can give it to him, but I know You can meet his need through me."

As I have shared this way of thinking with some, they have reacted with indignation. "God and sex don't mix," is the attitude I get. I wonder who they think created male and female and told them to populate the earth? God designed the sexual experience to take place between a married man and woman, and intended that it would be mutually satisfying for both. When I began to include God in that part of my life, He honored that and, through time, healed me of the emotional damage from the sexual abuse and enabled me freely and willingly to give myself to my husband. Today, as I write this, I can honestly say to you that I look forward to our times of intimacy. It is a true joy to share that part of the marriage relationship with someone who loves and accepts me for who I am.

This did not happen overnight for me, and it won't for you. Do not let yourself or anyone else tell you that in a certain time period you "should" be able to "get over it" and go on. This pulling-yourself-up-by-your-bootstraps advice kills. It condemns those who need more time to heal. This is also a piece of wrong advice given to couples healing from the effects of an affair. Often the offending partner thinks the spouse should heal faster then they are and accuses them of taking too long and causing more problems in the marriage because of it. These kinds of violations in a relationship cannot be healed by the calendar. The offended party deserves all the grace and time they need to mend, without condemnation.

PART II:

How To Disciple (love) Yourself and Others

INTRODUCTION

I am not a person with any educational titles, nor do I lay claim to great stores of knowledge. I share the following suggestions of how to disciple and mentor an abused person from the perspective of the victim, of one who has been discipled through the ravages of abuse, and now, of one who disciples. I share these truths with you, the victim, in the hope that you can find God's way of healing and then pass it on to those He will lead into your life who have experienced a similar violation.

11 ABUSE EQUALS

Abuse, be it physical, emotional, verbal, spiritual or sexual, *equals* traumatic life-altering rejection. *Perceived* abuse in any of these forms *equals* traumatic life-altering rejection. Actual and perceived abuse have the same effect on a person's life because the emotional trauma feels the same. This can make it very hard for a victim to discern the truth about what actually happened to them.

It is often true that what one person perceives as gross abuse is interpreted as minimal abuse by another, and vice versa. It can be difficult for an abused person to believe that anyone else has ever experienced the level of trauma that they have.

All this is to suggest that each individual and their personal experience must be treated as unique. Be on guard! Do not fall into the trap of comparison. Well-meaning disciplers and professionals alike tried to persuade me that my incident of abuse was not really that bad. "After all," they would say, "Look at all those who have been repeatedly abused or were actually raped. You were *lucky* that it wasn't worse than it was."

This seemingly rational approach created a very adverse reaction in me. Instead of thinking, "Whew! You're right, I was *lucky,*" and letting it go, I became consumed with increasingly heavy guilt and shame. I assumed there was something wrong with me. I must not be the Christian I thought I was. I was not able to slough it off, feel "lucky," and "let go and let God." I felt like I was being asked to deal with the abuse by the "instant potato" method—just add God, stir and POOF! No more pain and rejection! Sharing the details of my own sexual abuse with others often enables them to open up and share their details with me. This enables each of us to give honest validity to our own personal experience and removes the tendency to compare.

It is very important to be aware of your body language when you are listening to someone's story of abuse. Body language can reject a person as quickly as words. The people who share with me watch to see how I am going to react. Be sensitive, be real, be accepting, and more than anything else, show God's love. In other words, do for others as you would like them to do for you.

Because of who God is and how he gifts His children, you do not have to feel hindered in ministering to an abused person if you have never experienced abuse yourself. Being an open, willing vessel for the Holy Spirit to operate through you is the most important thing. Every day in my couseling ministry, I encounter people who have had far different experiences than I. It is a joy to watch God minister to these hurting individuals through me. I do not have to feel any lack because I have been spared the same pain.

Chapter

12 Now What Do I Say?

Romans 8:28 is a familiar verse: "And we know that in all things God works for the good of those who love Him, who have been called according to His purpose." Frequently, when Christians don't know what to say to a hurting sister or brother, they quote this verse. Yet what the hurting individual often hears is, "Yes, you have been hurt and rejected, but God is in control, so get over it," or, "This is just something you are going to have to accept. Get on with your life. It must have been God's will; after all, God is sovereign, and nothing happens unless He allows it." Even worse, I have heard some well-meaning Christians say, "God caused this for your good, so just accept it and learn a lesson from it."

I will freely admit that, in a twisted sort of way, these things have an element of truth about them. The meaning in the Greek text of Romans 8:28 implies that *"in the midst of all things"* God is working for our good. In other words, He is on our side no matter what is going on in our life. Yet, when this verse is quoted to some people, it is like a slap in the face. It can be like saying to a person who has just had their leg amputated, "This was God's will for you, so you have no right to be sad, depressed or angry. God did this for your good, so be glad for it and get on with your life." This communicates to the victim that their feelings of pain and violation are *wrong*. This, in turn, begins a vicious spiral of guilt, denial, anger and depression that can last a lifetime.

Even though I have been a discipler for over ten years now, I sometimes don't know what to say to a broken person who has just shared their life's hurts with me. When that happens, I don't

41

say anything. All too often people operate under the misconception that because they are a Christian they should be able to give a profoundly spiritual answer to another's problems -- an answer which will catapult them into a new way of handling their pain, and thus straighten out their life for good.

I know from personal experience that I was not looking for answers; I was looking for love and acceptance. In the beginning I simply needed someone to hold my hand and cry with me; someone to share my anger; someone who would not shy away and avoid me the next time we met; someone who would call a few days later and sincerely ask how I was doing, and *really* want to know.

It is odd to me how differently mankind treats the physically *ill* as opposed to victims of emotional, physical, spiritual and sexual *abuse*.

I have done a lot of hospital ministry. I have slept on the floor of many a hospital room for nights on end with a scared, pregnant mother whose baby was in distress. I have held the still-born son of a young couple and cried inconsolable tears with them. I have sat by the bedside of someone wasting away from cancer, feeling totally helpless. In all these times it never occurred to me to tell any of these people to just "Buck up, things will get better if you don't dwell on your present circumstances." Neither did it occur to me to tell them, "This is something you will never get over. Don't expect your life ever to be happy again." Yet, I have discipled countless abused persons who have been told both of these things, by professionals and well-meaning Christians alike.

When the victim is playing "victim heal thyself," they will tell themselves these things, too. I know I did. I would often beat myself up for not being able to "let go and let God," not taking into consideration that I had absolutely no idea how to do it.

I believe that "self-talk" is one of the most powerful tools we possess, whether for good or for evil. As a victim, I have the power to talk myself into being calm by using the Word of God to fill my mind, thus giving me something else to meditate on rather than the hurt and pain of my violation. Just the opposite is true as well. I can talk myself into a state of anxiety and fear by dwelling on the details of the abuse.

As victims and mentors alike, we must choose to deal with the moment. Give yourself and other hurting individuals the freedom to hurt. Do not labor under the misconception that you have to have an answer for yourself or others, or that an answer is even necessary at the moment.

As mentors or disciplers, when someone shares their pain with you, don't try to "fix" it. Just pray, and ask God to give you the ability to enter into their pain with them. Ask for the gift of empathy [emotional identification; understanding; compassion], and do all you can to reject the urge to show sympathy [condolence; fellow feelings]. Remember, you do not have to have experienced the same pain and circumstances to empathize with someone. That is one of the wonderful things about being *born of the Spirit of God*. He has perfect empathy with each one of us, no matter what the circumstances. He will gladly impart His empathy to you as you sincerely choose to give of yourself by showing love and acceptance to the one sharing with you.

Fear, guilt, and lack of peace are often bedfellows for abused persons. When ministering to victims of abuse, one of the most well-received things I do (when appropriate) is hold the individual. I always ask first. Some are so afraid of being touched; yet safe, loving touch is what they need and crave the most. It may begin with just holding their hand and praying, or a pat on the back, or a hug.

Of course, I do not hold men. I do ask them if they would like to be held by another man. On rare occasions, when my husband or another man is with me, a man may need to be held by me. God often uses me to represent a mother figure to people. Men who have been abused by women sometimes need to be held by a woman. I happen to be comfortable with that. If you are a woman in ministry and are not, that is perfectly okay. I encourage you to draw men into your ministry who can be comfortable holding other men. If you are a man in ministry, search for women to come alongside you to be available to hold another women. The touch is a powerful instrument of healing. It is no wonder that a recent article I read about working with victims of anorexia states that they are finding that sitting and holding these precious individuals for hours on end is bringing about great progress in their healing. During physical or sexual abuse, the abused person receives the message, "I must deserve being treated this way." An appropriate, safe, loving touch can override that message. But pray before you reach out to touch such a person; allowing your touch is risky to them.

13 WHO AM I?

Many victims of abuse often tend to draw their identity from their abusive past. I was no different, and possibly neither are you or those you are discipling. The emotional devastation of abuse became the foundation of my identity. Once I remembered the incident, it became the justification for all the bad things that happened to me. I felt I deserved them all. I walked around with a chip on my shoulder, looking for reasons to validate how miserable I felt. If anything good came into my life I felt I deserved it too, because of the abuse I had suffered. Yet, in the middle of the night I would turn around and reject the good that had happened to me because, after all, I was a soiled human being and didn't really deserve it. I was a very confused individual. The memory of the abuse gave me a reason (in truth, an excuse) to blame my pain and misery on someone else.

At first all the blame was on the shoulders of the perpetrator. As I progressed though my journey of self-pity and self-condemnation, I began to blame anyone and everyone around me; I was unwilling to take any personal responsibility for my attitudes and actions. After all, they hadn't walked a mile in my moccasins and didn't really understand my pain. I was tired of hearing how much God loved me and how He wanted to heal my pain and give me the ability to move on with my life! The truth was, I was so angry at God that there was no way I could grasp the concept that He loved me.

I am so thankful that God led a soft-spoken, yet persistent, mentor into my life. She showed that she loved me and accepted me in a thousand ways. It took time for me to learn to trust her. I was afraid. She knew everything about me! I protected myself from possible repeated rejection by emotionally holding myself back from listening to her gentle, consistent, persistent words.

The answer came when I began to listen for the first time to what she was saying. I allowed her to lead me gently into a clear understanding of who Jesus is, and who I am in Him. Only when I was willing to give up my victim-centered identity in exchange for my Christ-centered identity did I experience the healing of the violation of my personhood. This was the only way that I was able, once and for all, to lay down the pain and rejection and go forward. Recognizing Christ's life within me enabled me to experience His freedom and victory.

What does it mean to allow Jesus Christ to live His life through you? Galatians 2:20 says it clearly: "I have been crucified with Christ and I no longer live, but Christ lives in me. The life I live in the body, I live by faith in the Son of God, who loved me and gave Himself for me." Jesus was innocent of any wrongdoing, yet He was crucified. He chose to take on my sin, my pain, and my violation. He allowed Himself to be beaten beyond recognition, to be nailed to a tree and pierced in the side, so that I might have a life of peace, love and acceptance (Isaiah 53:4-5).

Anyone who loved me this much deserved the benefit of the doubt in my life. I came to realize that, instead of blaming God for what had happened to me, I had every reason to thank Him for protecting me in the midst of the violation (Psalm 91).

It was not God's will for me to be sexually abused. It was not God's will that any of the hurt and pain on this earth should happen. Yet He chose, before the foundation of the world, to give mankind a free will and not to override that free will. The family friend who violated me is the one who was at fault. It was his choice to hurt me, not God's! God allowed that man to exercise his free will, but God Himself was there with me the whole time. He experienced the same violation I did because He chose not to leave me or forsake me (Hebrews 13:5b).

As a believer I have given my life over to my Lord. It truly is no longer I who now live. I have chosen to give God permission to live His life through me. Therefore, I have begun to see that the abuse was not *my* abuse, but *our* abuse. Whatever happened to me, happened to my Lord. He chose to be that intimate with me.

The only personal experience I can relate it to is being a parent. Only a mother can understand another mother's fears, joys and love for her child. Only a father can really understand another father's desire for his child to succeed in his/her chosen career. It is a deeply intimate, shared experience that cannot be wholly understood outside of like roles. It is that way with God and me. He is the only one who can *truly* understand my abuse experience because He is the only one who wholly shared it with me.

Only when I came to understand this concept of God (the concept that He is a God of His word, a God of His commitment to love, accept, care for and protect me *in* my pain, before, during and after) did I begin to experience true peace for the first time in my life. Psalm 139 brought this truth home to me. I encourage you to read it out loud. Wherever a personal pronoun appears (i.e., *me, I*), put your name in its place. "O Lord, you have searched Cheryl and You know Cheryl..." I pray that this exercise will have the same soothing, healing effect on you that it had on me.

I recommend that you read Neil T. Anderson's book, *Victory Over The Darkness.* This book changed my life. It clearly showed me who I am in Christ and how to appropriate this new understanding into my daily routine. I began to understand the concept that whatever is true about Jesus is true about me. That is, because I have received salvation, I have received all of the character traits of Jesus, and I am now a co-heir with Him in eternity (Romans 8:17).

Dr. Anderson has included in his book a list of Scriptures called the WHO I AM list. The passages listed concentrate on the attributes and character of God. I encourage you to take one fact off the list each day and meditate on it. I call these my "one-a-day spiritual vitamins." The more of these facts you learn, the more you will be able to set your mind on God's truth about you and Him, no matter what your emotions are doing.

Scripture is clear that we can only truly love another to the degree we love ourselves. I shared in my story about God asking me why I would subject someone I love to a relationship with someone I hate. I think this is far more true about the general population then anyone wishes to admit. Self-love is a very important thing to God. He told us to love others AS we love ourselves. As? Yes. Mirror image. In the same way we love ourselves we are to show love to others. Ouch! Turn this around and it really means that we are unable to love others in any way except the way in which we love ourselves. Each of us needs to take a long hard look inside and ask the question, "How do I show love to myself? Is this the way I want to show love to those around me?"

Jesus loved himself. He knew exactly who He was and never felt the need to defend Himself to anyone. He did not have to be a people-pleaser to find acceptance in the eyes of His earthly peers. He knew that His total acceptance came from the Father. His identity was wrapped up in who He was, not how He performed. So is yours. I pray that you will find your acceptance and love for yourself in your Father's eyes and that it will be enough to satisfy your soul.

Chapter

14 Forgiving Correctly

A major issue that all abused persons must face is coming to the place where they can forgive the perpetrator. Oh! I can just see the hair rising on the back of your neck! You are probably saying, "Forgive him/her? You've got to be kidding!"

God wonderfully prepared me for this issue of forgiveness, before He revealed my abuse to me. I had just been through several weeks of Bible study on the subject and had a fresh perspective on it. You may have noticed that I chose to forgive my perpetrator right at the beginning. I knew that was what I was supposed to do, but I had no idea how long it would take me to deal with the feelings related to the abuse.

Why did I title this chapter FORGIVING *CORRECTLY*? Because, oddly enough, many Christians have a false idea of what forgiveness really is and how to do it in a way that brings true release and freedom. It is not uncommon to hear someone say, "If you are still angry at the one who hurt you, you haven't really forgiven them;" or, "If you are not able to forget the wrong done to you, you haven't forgiven the one who did it."

I was caught up in these kinds of deceptions. I had been taught that forgiveness was based on how I felt. In other words, if I was still feeling angry and hurt, then I had not forgiven the perpetrator; conversely, if I no longer felt angry or hurt, I had forgiven him.

No! Forgiveness is not based on feelings. It is a discretionary act of the will, a cold, hard choice. Forgiveness is (Matthew 18:21-35):

1. An undeserved gift.
2. Erasing or forgoing what is due, canceling the debt owed, and giving up all claims to compensation. This Scripture also makes it clear that, once forgiveness is received from God, it is to be passed on to others.

Now let's clear up what forgiveness is *not* . Forgiveness is *not* not feeling angry anymore. Remember, it is not based on feelings. When you choose to forgive someone for the wrong they have done to you, you need to do it simply because God commanded you to, and the sooner the better! But you will probably still be in the throes of the emotional experience of the violation, as I was. You then pray, giving God permission to move you through the emotional upheaval. Ask Him to bring your emotions in line with your decision to forgive. You need to be aware that sometimes your emotions may not change. This does not mean that God isn't answering your prayer, or that you are doing something wrong. It simply means that your emotions are doing their own thing. Forgiveness has still taken place. It is a fact.

An illustration of this truth comes from the kitchen. When you put a large pot of water on the stove and turn the burner up to high, it takes the water several minutes to come to a full boil. What happens when you turn the burner off? Does the water immediately stop boiling? No! It takes time; and it takes even more time for the water to cool down to the temperature at which it started. Your emotions are like the boiling water. When you are obedient and choose to forgive someone who has hurt you, you are turning off the "burner" under your emotions. They are no longer being fueled by unforgiveness, but it will take them a while to cool down to their level prior to the violation. Just accept that you have chosen to be in line with God's will for you by forgiving; then allow His love and acceptance of you to be sufficient, and give your emotions time to heal.

50

NEWS FLASH! Your emotions are never right and they are never wrong—but they are always valid. They are God-given. Without them you would be unable to have a fulfilling relationship with God or any human being.

Through the years the Lord has taught me to talk to my emotions, rather than letting my emotions talk to me. By this I mean that He has taught me how not to let my emotions control me. When I am feeling upset and my emotions are rising, I say something like this, "Anger, I know you are there. That is okay, but you are not going to control my thoughts and actions. I am a child of the King, filled with His Spirit, and I choose to think about all that is true about me because of my relationship to my Savior." Then I set my mind on the facts of who God says I am in Christ -- my one-a-day spiritual vitamins. I am still feeling angry, but the anger is not controlling my thoughts and causing me to do and say sinful things.

Forgiveness is *not* trying to justify, understand or explain away someone's rejective behavior. It is *not* making excuses for the perpetrator.

Forgiveness is *not* forgetting. We do not forget. Only God says He will forget our sins once we have confessed them to Him.

Forgiveness is *not* denying that we have really been hurt, or pretending that the hurt was really not that big a thing. This is called stuffing your emotions. Believe me, I know from personal trauma: stuffed emotions will come back to haunt you.

Forgiveness does *not* mean that the broken relationship must be restored. The man who violated me still lives in my small Alaskan town, but I have never sensed the leading of God to be friends with him. We have all read or heard of cases where the person who was wronged has befriended the one who committed the violation against them or a member of their family. These are real accounts of forgiveness in action, but don't put yourself or God in a box and assume that you have to do it the same way. Forgiveness is the decision we make to free ourselves from the ossibility of becoming bitter and hard, which would only harm us. Your only job in the forgiveness process is to give God permission to decide where it needs to go from there. If He wants you to be one of those who do develop a healthy relationship with the one who abused you, He will make that very clear to you. You do not have to initiate relationship to prove you have forgiven the abuser; your job is to be willing to have relationship if God so chooses.

In short, forgive *as* Christ forgave you and give Him control of whatever may happen next between you and the one you have forgiven.

Unforgiveness is the opposite of forgiveness and only results in personal torture and inner torment—not to mention the fact that it is a sin. In Matthew, chapter 6, Christians are admonished to forgive *as* we are forgiven, meaning "in the same way." The command to forgive knows no limitations. There is no violation so horrible that we are given permission to withhold forgiveness. Jesus is our example. He forgave those who nailed Him to the cross while He was still on the cross!

I chose to forgive my perpetrator at the beginning of my process. As you know, I still went through emotional torment; yet I feel certain in my heart that it was that act of forgiveness that enabled me to walk all the way through the healing process. It was the catalyst that enabled me not to get stuck in my grief, becoming consumed with bitterness and anger. I much prefer the peace that is present in my life today.

A very effective way to forgive someone is to sit down before an empty chair, mentally put the perpetrator in the chair and talk to the person face-to-face. Tell them how they hurt you, leaving out nothing. Tell them how the violation made you feel. Charge them with the emotional debt by being honest with your feelings.

Now comes the hard part! Verbally release the perpetrator from the debt they owe you. Tell them that they never have to make anything up to you. Make a clear decision of your will to accept the person unconditionally, just as they are. Release the person from the responsibility to make you feel loved and accepted. Only Jesus can meet this need for security and significance in you. Then lastly, be willing, before God, to be hurt again if He allows it. It is a sad reality that we hurt, and are hurt by those we love.

So, what if the same person hurts you again? Forgive them and keep their account at zero. Forgiveness makes reconciliation possible. In other words, don't keep a record of wrong against anyone, including yourself.

I hope it goes without saying that if you are in a situation where you perceive you are currently being abused in any way, you need to seek outside counsel to determine the kind and extent of the abuse taking place and what you could be doing to actively change the situation. Forgiving repeated instances of abuse is the right thing to do, but it does not mean that you should stay in an abusive environment.

What if the person never changes? Hallelujah! That is God's problem!

What if you forgive and your feelings don't change, as I mentioned before? Believe it or not, that is God's problem, too! You need only to pray and affirm before God that you have chosen to forgive the person for the wrong committed. Ask God to bring your emotions in line with the fact that you have already forgiven the person, and trust Him for the timing.

There is probably no one in your life that you won't have to forgive sometime for something. Don't forget yourself. We are repeatedly our own worst enemy! We usually keep a much longer record of wrong against ourselves than we do against others. Put yourself in the empty chair and offer forgiveness to someone who desperately needs it.

Chapter

15 GOOD GRIEF!

Throughout my years of discipling I have come to understand grief in a different light. In the past I only associated grief with the death of a person. Now I realize that grief is a part of life. Grief comes whenever change happens in a person's life. Oh, I am not talking about the deep, wrenching emotional pain that comes when you suffer the loss of a loved one; I am talking about the sadness, the tugging at the heart when change intersects with life. We hear all the time that change is good. I believe that; yet even good, sought-after change can cause a person to grieve, to feel sadness and loss over things left behind.

Likewise, grief is experienced when violation of one's personhood occurs. When someone has been abused, or perceives that they have been abused, they grieve over the losses they have suffered. I grieved over the loss of my childhood and my innocence. I didn't know it at the time, but when I blocked the abuse out of my conscious mind, I was acting out my grief. Denial is one of the ways in which our mind and emotions handle severe shock and trauma.

When ministering to an abused person, one of the most beneficial things you can do for them is to teach them what grief is and how to grieve. I believe that the grief process is a God-given tool to enable mankind to progress emotionally through losses of all kinds.

Loss can happen in a person's life externally through death of a loved one, divorce, the loss of a job or loss of health. Internally, loss can occur when a person feels a lack of self-worth or self-confidence, loss of control, loss of security or the loss of their primary role in life. When these kinds of losses occur, a person may feel emotionally numb or in shock. Shock often triggers denial. ("I can't believe it. He can't be dead!" "I couldn't have been fired. I'll wake up and it will all be a bad dream." "This couldn't have happened to me!")

Denial buffers the person from reality. It temporarily protects the person from having to deal with the full reality of the circumstance all at once. They may feel paralyzed emotionally, physically and spiritually. The little three-year-old Cheryl who was violated out in the field that day, without ever consciously choosing to do so, entered into denial. Her little emotional being had no other way to deal with the trauma. That denial lasted for two decades because she had no idea it was a part of her life.

Loss, producing shock, handled through denial, brings on depression. Depression is a normal and necessary part of the grief process. It creates a sense of isolation. The person feels that no one has ever experienced the grief they are experiencing. Oftentimes the person believes that not even God can understand, and He doesn't really care anyway.

After God revealed the abuse to my conscious mind and I had moved out of the denial stage of my grief, I plummeted into deep depression. I realize now that I had been depressed, to some degree, most of my life. Even though I had no keen memory of the abuse, I reacted to it just the same.

I said that depression is a normal and necessary part of the grief process. Why? Because a person needs time to pull away from the emotional demands on their life and, so to speak, lick their wounds for a while. A person needs to become friends with their loss. I know this sounds silly, but it is very important. Let me explain.

Loss, especially when it is unwanted, undeserved or uncontrolled, causes a person to feel guilt. There is realistic guilt. This is guilt based on fact, guilt that produces godly sorrow. Godly sorrow then causes a person to repent of what they did wrong, receive God's forgiveness and go on with their life (2 Corinthians 7:8-11).

Then there is neurotic guilt, or false guilt. This brand of guilt drives a person crazy. Why? Because it is not based on fact. It is a feeling inside a person that makes them think they did something wrong but they can't figure out what it was.

I suffered from a lot of neurotic guilt over my son's health problems. He was sick; I was his mother. I couldn't fix him, no matter what I did. Doctors and health professionals were telling me it was my fault; why shouldn't I believe them? Yet later, when he was correctly diagnosed, I knew that it was not my fault, and there was nothing I could have done to make him feel better.

I experienced loads of neurotic guilt over not being able to freely give myself to David. After all, I reasoned, he was not the one who violated me. He loved me. Therefore, I must have been the one who was at fault.

I was on an emotional roller coaster with no off switch! I was full of anger and self-loathing. I resented anyone who had a good marriage. I resented anyone who tried to help me. My anger had become grossly displaced, but I didn't know it. I was afraid of the intense emotions I was expressing and didn't know how to handle them. The only thing to do was to try to control them; in other words, stuff them. This caused me to go back into a measure of denial. The only way I could ignore all these glaring feelings and circumstances was to deny they existed. So, unknown to me, I had become blocked in my grief.

Out of desperation I would invent excuses to take the children to my mother's and go off by myself. I would feel guilty, believing myself to be a horrible mother, but I would do it nonetheless. I know now it was the Lord nudging me into places of solitude: places where I would have to look my life in the face; times when I would not be able to escape the reality of what had happened to me. It was during these interludes that I began to embrace my suffering. I took hold of the facts of what had hap-

pened in my life and wrestled with them. I became familiar with
them instead of blocking them out. I became friends with my
losses. Little by little they didn't seem so overpowering any more.
The intensity of the emotional response began to lessen as I allowed myself to experience the emotions surrounding the abuse.

The most common response to loss is to stuff the intense
emotions and pretend it was not as bad as it could have been.
Anger denied becomes depression. Depression denied fuels guilt.
Misunderstood guilt fuels anxiety because the loss can not be
explained or reasoned out in logical terms, making it impossible
to find closure to the loss. This in turn rekindles the anger, which
must be suppressed because, to most people, anger is an unacceptable emotion. And round and round we go, and truly, where
the emotional pain stops, nobody knows.

I am always telling people to give themselves permission
to be who they are one day at a time. By this I mean that we need
to acknowledge our emotions, give them permission to be part
of our life and give ourselves permission to express those emotions in a way that will not harm ourselves or others. Remember
I said earlier that your emotions are not ever right or wrong, but
are always valid. No one, including yourself, has the right to tell
you that your emotional response to something is wrong. True,
your emotional response can be inappropriate or out of propor-
tion to the incident. You can choose to act out the emotions in a
way that is harmful to yourself, to another person, or to a relationship. This does not invalidate the emotion. It simply means
that you allowed the emotion to control your thoughts and actions, and perhaps your tongue.

The Lord Jesus Christ wants to be your example in everything. He had full expression of His emotions at all times. He
wept. He was angry. He was frustrated. Did He sin? No. He did
not let His emotions control His thoughts and actions, but neither did He deny them or stuff them. The reason we were given
emotions by God was so that we could be a relational being, first
with God, second with each other. Our emotions were not given

to us to measure how good or bad life is, or to control circumstances or relationships. When I finally understood this it brought me great freedom and peace. By making friends with my emotions, I was drawn closer to the time when I would be able to thank God for revealing the abuse to me in His time. 1 Corinthians 4:5 states that we are to *wait on the Lord*. He is the one who will bring to light what is hidden in darkness. I waited on Him and He exposed the darkness in my life, for my good. It was the only way for me to walk in liberty and live in harmony with myself, my past and my God.

This brings us to the final stage of the grief process: acceptance. When we have suffered the loss, moved through the shock, denial, depression, guilt and anger, we can begin to reaffirm life as it is. We can then choose to live in the reality of what has happened to us. We begin to realize that we can never go back. We can never relive those times of violation and have them come out with a different ending. We can never recapture the things we have lost along the way. In short, we will never be the same, nor should we want to be.

Loss produces change. We cannot stop it. We have two choices. We can become either a stronger person or a weaker person. We can choose to depend wholly on God and believe that He will love us through the pain, thus coming out a stronger person with resources to handle the next loss; or we can reject God's love and care and wallow in our misery, becoming weaker and weaker in every way.

If we choose God's way, we will at some point, be able to talk about the incident without having to succumb to the emotional devastation felt at the beginning. We will be able to talk about the loss in an objective way, enabling us to mentor others through the same process we went through. We go on, able to reconstruct life with a purpose, a life worth living again, with a sense of closure filling our soul.

Chapter

16 Praise Works!

The best antidote I know of for fear, anxiety, pain and feelings of helplessness is praise. I know that it works in my own life. I have put it to the test many times over the years. I have learned that there is no need that I cannot pray about in the form of praise. Instead of asking for so much, I simply praise God that He is already aware of the need and is taking care of it as we speak.

In 1 Thessalonians 5:16-18, God sums up exactly how He wants us to live our lives. He says, "Be joyful always; pray continually; give thanks in all circumstances, for this is God's *will* for *you* in Christ Jesus." It can't get much plainer than that!

What God is talking about is lifestyle. Joy, prayer and thankfulness should be our lifestyle. They should be the foundation from which we approach every aspect of our lives. I know, it is more easily said than done a good share of the time, especially if you are hurting or angry; but it is possible, or God would not have said it.

It is possible, but only if you choose to do it, no matter what your feelings or circumstances are. If you were to do a study of the great men and women of the Bible, I believe that you would find each one of them living this 1 Thessalonians 5:16-18 lifestyle—maybe not in the beginning, but definitely as they grow in their trust and love for God.

Jehoshaphat, in 2 Chronicles, Chapter 20, is a good example. He had three kings and their armies coming to destroy his kingdom. Verse 3 says, "Alarmed, Jehoshaphat *resolved* (chose) to inquire of the Lord..." As you read on you see that he didn't fall on his knees in fear, begging God to deliver them. No, he rose up before the assembly and proclaimed the goodness of the Lord. He praised God for all the times He had delivered them in the past. Then he brought his petition before the Lord. Notice how he phrased it. In verses 10 and 11 he reminded God that they had been faithful to obey Him and not destroy these three kingdoms when they came to this land. Then, in verse 12, he declares his position before God in this dilemma. "O our God, will you not judge them? For we have *no* power to face this vast army that is attacking us. We do *not* know what to do, *but* our eyes are on You."

Oh, how I can relate to that declaration! How many times during the healing process of my sexual abuse did I feel powerless? How often did I cry out to God that I didn't know what else to do? And oh, how sweet it was when I came to the place when I put my eyes on Him and trusted Him for my deliverance!

As we read the rest of the chapter we see how God handled the situation. He told them twice, in verses 15 and 17, not to be afraid or discouraged. In these verses He told them why. "...For the battle is *not* yours, but God's... You will not have to fight this battle. Take up your positions; stand firm and see the deliverance the Lord will give you."

God is in charge of the timing. He will do what He wills, when He wills it. There is nothing you can do to speed up or slow down God's deliverance! He is never late, and He is never early. Jehoshaphat knew this. He didn't wait for the actual deliverance to take place. He fell with his face to the ground and praised God for something he had not yet received (2 Chronicles 20:18-22). That is faith in action. "Now faith is being *sure* of what we hope for and *certain* of what we do not see. This is what the ancients were commended for." (Hebrews 11:1-2)

There is precedent for praise in the whole Bible. From page one to the end, God is continually admonishing His creation to praise Him. He said that if the Israelites did not praise Him the rocks would cry out. Why? Is God so egotistical that He has to be adulated all the time? Of course not! He said it over and over because he knows that praising Him is giving Him free access into the wounded, scared places in our lives, the places He loves to be the most. Only then can His full love, grace, mercy and healing be an active part of our past, present and future.

God is anxious to be God for you! The best way you can allow Him to be all that He wants to be on your behalf is to praise Him, no matter what. There is a wonderful book I recommend you invest in to help you develop a lifestyle of praise. It is *Thirty-One Days Of Praise*, by Ruth Myers. If you choose to take this concept seriously, this book will propel you into a fresh rewarding way of approaching all of life, and it will teach you how to praise for all your needs.

Chapter

17 WORD OF CAUTION

The aftermath of severe trauma can sneak up on you when you least expect it.

As I write this, it has been almost forty-five years since I was sexually molested. I confess to you that as I started to write the beginning of this story, telling the details of the abuse, I had to stop several times because of the memories of the emotional pain I felt. Remembering that little three-year-old, whose blind trust for her friend caused her to be grossly used, brought tears to my eyes.

About six years ago I encountered the man who had violated me. I had not seen him for many years and was shocked to see him. As I saw him walking by, I was filled with anger toward him. I thought, "He looks as though he has never done anything evil in his life! How dare he come back here!" All of a sudden I felt very afraid. What if he hadn't changed and was still doing the same kind of horrible things to little girls, or women? I turned and ran as fast as I could, my heart pounding so hard I thought it would jump out of my chest. It took me several days to calm down. I prayed through the emotions, and allowed the Lord to focus my thinking in His direction. I did not go to the man and shake his hand and tell him it was nice to see him, but neither was I afraid or bitter when I encountered him the next time.

It is uncanny the things that will trigger memories in our mind: a smell, a certain color, a particular sound or the chance sighting of the back of someone in a crowd who reminds you of the one who hurt you. Sometimes even now, if I am caught by surprise when my husband reaches for me in the night, I will flinch and shrink back from his touch. But it doesn't last, and it no longer hinders our relationship.

Sometimes when I am out walking I will see a man coming toward me and feel anxiety rising in me. I look to see if there are cars in any of the driveways and lights on in the houses. I take a few deep breaths, remind myself that I am not walking alone because my Lord hasn't left me, and I go on, praising God for His tender love and protection.

Our home burned to the ground when I was in high school. It was several hours before I knew whether my parents had been in the fire. When I see a home burning on TV, or hear of someone I know who has suffered that loss, my heart constricts. But after thirty-two years, I no longer keep my keepsakes in a box by the door like I used to.

No, you don't ever forget, but you do grow into acceptance of the things you cannot change. You grow in your ability to trust your heavenly protector with your whole life, past, present and future. You remember, but you don't obsess. You recall, but you don't suffer the loss over and over again. You recollect, but you do not allow the loss to control your mind, emotions and will.

The way to lasting freedom from the ravages of any form of abuse is through receiving Jesus Christ as your Savior, and then learning how to make Him your Lord. This comes through understanding your flesh, sometimes called sinful nature, those things you are using to make life work outside of Jesus Christ and His character. Your flesh will always need to self-promote and self-protect. Because Christ Jesus is your protection, your source of happiness, peace and contentment -- in short, your source for life -- you need to surrender the right to make your life work out of your own self-sufficiency. Give God permission to be your sufficiency, your all in all. In truth, He is your sufficiency, whether you act like He is or not; so why not make the choice and life-change to enter into what is already true about you? Come under God's ALL-sufficient protection and provision. And above all, remind yourself that what your enemy, Satan, meant for your harm, God has turned all around and is using for your good and the good of others who can benefit from your experience. Your emotions may not be at a place where they agree that your abuse experience is working toward your good, but that is okay. Give God full freedom and time to heal your emotions and cause them to come in line with your mindset. Choose to take God at His word when He says that what was bondage has now been exchanged for freedom. What were lies have now been exchanged for truth; and truth has, and always will, set you free!

EPILOGUE

I have found that each time I share with someone about my abuse experience and the healing God has done in my life I experience a greater measure of joy. Would I change my life, if I could, to omit the sexual abuse? I believe I would, knowing that God is sufficient to give me compassion for others without having had to experience the same thing. Yet now, having gone through it, I can praise God because of the wonderful way in which He equipped me to minister to others in all walks of life. I believe I have a bit more patience, empathy, understanding and grace for others because of what I have personally experienced. Somehow it makes my pain have meaning and purpose it may not otherwise have had.

If you are a victim of abuse I sincerely hope that this book has been an instrument of God's healing love on your journey to freedom. I would love to hear from you. If you have not found someone with whom you feel safe sharing your experience, perhaps I can help. If you are ministering to an abused person, my desire is that you have gained in knowledge, empathy, patience and grace to the benefit of those you are discipling. God Bless.

Cheryl Zumbrunnen

You are welcome to write with comments or questions at the address below.

Crossroads Ministries
P.O. Box 871831
Wasilla, AK 99687-1831

CRM

ADDITIONAL RESOURCES
BY THE AUTHOR

PUBLICATIONS

- MISCARRIAGE ... THE MISUNDERSTOOD DEATH
  Those grieving the loss of their <u>child</u> don't need the
  theological answers to their loss, they need self-sacrifing
  friends and family who will just be with them and
  listen.

- SATAN, THE DEFEATED ONE
  A scriptural study of the believer's authority and victory
  over Satan.

- PRAYER
  Learning how to cultivate an effective, powerful prayer
  life.

AUDIO CASSETTE
Music to Quiet the Troubled Soul

- TIMES OF PEACE

  Side 1: Nothin' Improves My Day, It All Depends,
  Living In The Presence, In This Very Room,
  Take This Broken Heart

  Side 2: We Are The Reason, Blinded Eyes, I'll Keep My Eyes On You,
  Jesus Will Still Be There, My Tribute

To receive information or to order resources from pages 68-69,
write to:

Crossroads Ministries
P.O. Box 871831
Wasilla, AK 99687-1831

CRM

68

CONFERENCE, WORKSHOP SEMINARS & RETREATS
OFFERED BY CROSSROADS MINISTRIES

CRM staff are experienced speakers who are available for travel to present seminars & retreats to your church or group.

- GRACELIFE CONFERENCE
  This conference is not about changing a Christian's life, but *exchanging* a self-centered life for a Christ-centered life and helping Christians discover and experience the real presence of JESUS CHRIST in all they are and all they do.

- GRACELIFE WORKSHOP
  (Pre-requisite: GraceLife Conference)
  This workshop is designed to give practical experiences in sharing some of the truths learned in the GraceLife Conference. The objectives are to deepen a believer's spiritual life (pastors, counselors, teachers and lay people) and to equip them to effectively disciple/mentor others into the knowledge of, and walking in, their identity in Christ rather than in the flesh.

- ADDITIONAL RETREATS & SEMINARS
  David & Cheryl and the staff of Crossroads Ministries are eager and willing to minister to individuals in need as well as be available to do retreats and special speaking engagements on the topic of your choice.

SUGGESTED READING LIST

Act Of Marriage, Tim LaHay
Always Daddy's Girl, H. M. Wright
*The Bondage Breaker, Neil T. Anderson
Christian's Secret of A Happy Life, Hanna Whitall Smith
*Confident Woman, Anabel Gillham
For Those Who Hurt, Chuck Swindoll
Gift of Forgiveness, Charles Stanley
Healing For Damaged Emotions, David Seamonds
Stillness In The Storm, Anabel Gillham
*Thirty-One Days Of Praise, Ruth Myers
*Victory Over The Darkness, Neil T. Anderson

SUGGESTED AUDIO TAPES

Exchanged Life Conference, Lee LeFebre
   (8 Tape Album)
Hope For The Abused, Wilkinson, Best, Cabot
*Victory Series IV, Jack Taylor
   (4 Tape Album)

*These are resources I use often in discipleship/counseling.

Resources are available through:
   CROSSLIFE EXPRESSIONS BOOK STORE
   10610 E. Bethany Drive, Suite A
   Aurora, Co 80014

   Orders may also be faxed (303) 750-1228, or be placed
   by calling 1-800-750-6818.

Should books or tapes not be available at the above bookstore,
check at your local Christian Book Store.